D1222183

1. Self Portrait of the artist c. 1922.

T.

JOHN BUTLER YEATS AND THE IRISH RENAISSANCE BY JAMES WHITE WITH PICTURES FROM THE COLLECTION OF MICHAEL BUTLER YEATS AND FROM THE NATIONAL GALLERY OF IRELAND

THE DOLMEN PRESS

CONTENTS

Acknowledgement is made to An Chomhairle Ealaíon (The Arts Council of Ireland) for their assistance in the production of this book.

General Editor : Liam Miller

Printed and published in the Republic of Ireland at the Dolmen Press, 8 Herbert Place, Dublin 2. First published in 1972. Distributed outside Ireland, except in the United States of America and in Canada, by Oxford University Press.
Distributed in the United States of America by Humanities Press Inc., 450 Park Avenue South, New York, NY 10016.

PADRAIC COLUM

THE PAINTER

JOHN BUTLER YEATS

'To-night,' you said, 'to-night all Ireland round
The curlews call.' The dinner-talk went on
And I knew what you heard and what you saw,
That left you for a little while withdrawn —
The lonely land, the lonely-crying birds!

Your words, your breath are gone!
O uncaught spirit, we'll remember you
By those remote and ever-flying birds
Adown the Shannon's reach, or crying through
The mist between Clew Bay and Dublin Bay!

Your words, your breath are gone,
I, careless, said. But your live eyes, live hand
Have left the pictures of these noted men,
So many, and so filled with wakefulness
That voices from them pass above the land.

from Irish Elegies, The Dolmen Press, Dublin

I THE MIND OF THE ARTIST

More is known about the way John Butler Yeats's mind worked in relation to the problems and nature of art than is known about most painters who ever lived. This is due to the preservation of his many illuminating letters and of course, in greatest part, to his gifts as a philosopher and writer.

Yet the idea is frequently put forward that the artist who can only communicate in one medium is the better for being forced to direct all his attention to his chosen metier. If it be possible to make an exception I do so in the case of John Butler Yeats (to whom I will after this refer as JBY as it prevents confusion with his sons). He was a portrait painter. All his life he was engaged in an encounter with the personality of his sitter. He knew exactly what he wanted to do. It was to capture the moment of illumination in a gesture or expression; to set down a glimpse of humanity in a smile; to enlarge experience by showing us a living being in a pencil sketch or an oil painting.

He realised the importance of the artist's position as an observer of concrete facts, and as a being capable of imaginative insight. A careful student of his writings will discover that he regarded the artist as an idealist requiring all the restraint of a saint when it came to material prosperity. He saw him nevertheless as an individual who must never pander to middleclass ideas of virtue or modesty, else he would become a mere recorder of appearances and the equivalent of an economist or a man of action.

By constantly searching for the moment of magic in terms of revealing his sitter's inner soul or radiance, he lived on the brink of success which never quite seemed to become fact. Yet he was an optimist who, year after year, wrote in his letters that success was just around the corner. When he died in New York he believed that he had left at least a few great portraits. He probably realised that few of his friends shared that view. But so real and intense was his understanding of the artistic process that his own conviction was closer to the objective truth than most observers might imagine.

The eldest of eight children, he was born on 16 March 1839 in the Parish of Tullylish, Co. Down, where his father was Rector. His happiness as a child he frequently recalled and he spoke of his father as his friend and his mother as his conscience. When he was a very little boy he spent two years at Seaforth, near Liverpool, at a school kept by two old maids. Later he went with his three brothers to a school in the Isle of Man, the Atholl Academy. When he entered Trinity College in Dublin in 1857 he was expected to follow the family tradition by studying for the church. However, he finally read Law and was called to the Bar in 1866, devilling for Isaac Butt, the politician friend of his father, whom he greatly admired. Meanwhile, on 10 September 1863, he married Susan Mary Pollexfen of Sligo and set up house in Sandymount where his son W. B. Yeats was born in 1865.

In 1867 he took his young wife and two-year-old son to London to commence his long life's apprenticeship to the business of being a portrait painter. His struggles and associations are gracefully described in the memoir by Joseph Hone which forms the introduction to the artist's letters to his son W. B. Yeats which were published by Faber & Faber, London, in 1944. With incredible stoicism he stood up to the criticisms of his wife's family, the deprivations attendant on continued failure to make a living and constant changes of residence, frequent returns by his family to their grandparents in Sligo, as well as many other disappointments in his endeavours to obtain employment as an illustrator and writer.

In fact it could hardly be said that he ever had any continued success or patronage, apart from the commission he received from Sir Hugh Lane in 1901 to portray leading figures in modern Irish history, and later in New York when friends like John Quinn obtained occasional commissions for him between 1908 and his death there in 1922.

In his excellent essay on *The Yeats Family and the Pollexfens of Sligo* published by The Dolmen Press in 1971, William M. Murphy clearly brings out the sweetness of his character and his capacity by a sort of divine charity to resist the material pressures of the Pollexfens into whom he had married and whose love of property and preference for class privilege seemed to him wholly undesirable tendencies.

Apart from his impracticality in the business of survival for himself and his family, JBY was a highly rational individual with an extremely rounded philosophy of life as it appeared to an artist. He seemed to regard man in this universe as a truly noble creature but he cared little for the formal values of science, religion or indeed any kind of orthodoxy. When he was a student at Trinity College he discovered 'without any sense of loss that he could not accept the supernatural'.[1] Gradually he seems to have immersed himself in the study of literature and art and the process of the mind of the artist. He considered that the artist must relinquish all hold on the practical ends of existence and direct his attention to the cultivation of the aesthetic. These notions seem to have attracted him with all the force which is normally applied by the religious in their desire for mystical experience.

As early as 1869 he wrote to Professor Dowden[2] 'It seems to me that the intellect of man as man, and therefore of an artist, the most human of all, should obey no voice except that of emotion, but I would have a man know all emotions. Shame, anger, love, pity, contempt, admiration, hatred, and whatever

9

other feelings there be, to have all those roused to their utmost strength, and to have all of them roused, (two things you observe), is the aim, as I take it, of the only right education.' He was referring here, he pointed out, to emotion, not in the sense of excitement but in the sense in which all feelings of which he is capable cause his senses to vibrate and to stimulate his inventive powers. Years later in 1914 in a letter to his son, WB from New York, he wrote: 'Once lecturing in Dublin I proposed that the word invitation should be substituted for temptation since we really came on earth to be tempted, and that in most cases it was our business not to resist but to yield to it and take the consequences, even thought it required the courage of a hero. St. Francis was a man of pleasure, who had gone the round of the passions. This was the history of all the great saints. It is only the great sinner who can do the two things of hating the sin and loving the sinner — the other sort only hate the sinner.'[3] This doctrine was later elaborated by André Gide in 'Later Fruits of the Earth' published by Secker & Warburg in 1935. Here JBY was concerned with the idea of man yielding himself up to the process of the artist's imagination. 'Art only comes when there is abandon, and a world of dreaming and waiting and passionate meditation.'[4] He believed that the artist must be capable of achieving universality of feelings: 'Love by itself is lust, that is primitive animalism, and anger what is it but homicide? Art lifts us out of the sphere of mere bestiality, art is a musician and touches every chord in the human harp — in other words a single feeling becomes a mood and the artist is a man with a natural tendency to thus convert every single feeling into a mood — he is a moody man.'[5]

The condition of mind which JBY saw as necessary to the creative artist was first of all the engendering of emotion which would produce the mood necessary for the work to be undertaken. He truly believed in the almost utopian attitude of sincerity and happiness and truth marking the character of the artist so that his attitudes would be reflected in the quality of his pictures.

> How ignoble beside this doctrine of sincerity, as much pagan as christian is the Puritan doctrine denouncing human nature as vile.[6]

Later he wrote

> Thus I come to the conclusion, that the only sincerity in a practical world is that of the artist. Hence the eternal dispute between them and the rulers of the world. If we speak at all, we must say what we believe otherwise our tongue is palsied. For which reason, artists, in the world's history, have, when they have been wise, always kept themselves apart. Napoleon hated literary men; he said they were merely manufacturers of phrases.[7]

On another occasion, reporting a lecture to an immense crowd of grim-faced men and women in Philadelphia, he recorded that 'he had the courage to tell the people in question that Puritanism was a mistake because it only permitted us to admire people, whereas the real thing is to love people.'[8]

His search for truth and sincerity was directed by his conviction that the artist was the sole guardian of essential values which were preserved by men like Shakespeare but ignored by the mighty rulers. He constantly railed against the puritan as against any other who would limit the capacity of man to expand his possibilities of joyful living. By continuously maintaining these points of view he was ensuring a consistency of outlook in himself which he knew would assist him in the pursuit of pictures which would always reflect the deepest human values and a sympathy essential to his whole existence.

Of course he went much further than just to insist on certain basic values. He also regarded the element of beauty as something the artist must garner from the harvest of experience. He frequently referred to the rose as a symbol of this beauty which he also allied with freedom. He recognised that certain elements like beauty could not be defined. 'If the rose puzzled itself over the question of how it grew, it would not be the miracle it is' he once said. Nevertheless he made a clear distinction between those who provided ideas and those who gave such ideas, true illumination or magic. Writing in the Irish Statesman in 1919 he made this lucid pronouncement:

> The Rose and its lover, the Nightingale, are one thing — and the cross-grained old Scotch gardener is another thing. And these do not in the least degree resemble each other, being of quite different species. And the rose and the nightingale, if they had not more important matters to think about, would know that the old gardener in his heart hates both of them, and would if he had his way turn the rose into a cabbage or a turnip or a radish; for there is no utility in the rose, or so he thinks, and his mind is bent on utility. All those uplift poets and uplift playwriters, G. B. Shaw and Ibsen — all of them — are like that gardener — they are just as indispensable. Without them there would be no poetry, as without the gardener the rose would not be the blooming creature it is. These playwriters and uplift poets think that poetry is their concern, and it is so, but indirectly. They do not themselves produce or create the poetical. Their task, to put it at its highest value, is to open the cage that the

bird may escape where it may sing its wildest; they themselves do not sing, that is for the bird, that is its business.

He believed that his son WB was, like himself, a songbird who must always be prepared to find wild song when the right moment would arise. The moment was of course the entry into dreamland.

The chief thing to know and never forget is that art is dreamland and that the moment a poet meddles with ethics and the moral uplift or thinking scientifically, he leaves dreamland, loses all his music and ceases to be a poet,

he wrote to WB in 1914. Later in the same letter he went on,

We all live when at our best, that is when we are most ourselves in dreamland. A man with his wife or child and loving them, a man in grief and yielding to it, girls and boys dancing together, children at play — it is all dreams, dreams, dreams. A student over his books, soldiers at the war, friends talking together — it is still dreamland — actual life on a far away horizon which becomes more and more distant. When the essential sap of life is arrested by anger or hatred we suddenly are aware of the actual, and music dies out of our hearts and voices — the anger subtly present in ethical thought — as it is also in most kinds of arguments : how many poems has it laid low ?

The poet is a magician — his vocation to incessantly evoke dreams and do his work so well, because of natural gifts and acquired skill, that his dreams shall have a

13

potency to defeat the actual at every point. Yet here is a curious thing, the poet and we his dupes know that they are only dreams — otherwise we lose them. With our eyes open, using our will and powers of selection, we, together in friendship and brotherly love, create this dreamland. Pronounce it to be actual life and you summon logic and mechanical sense and reason and all the other powers of prose to find yourself hailed back to the prison house, and dreamland vanishes — a shrieking ghost.[9]

JBY never had any doubt about the function of the artist to bring into existence a work which contained, like the rose, a special magic, and this he associated with the lyrical joy of those moved by emotion and association away from the prosaic acts of daily life. Some writers have referred to 'ecstasy' when, endeavouring to explain what JBY above calls 'dreamland'. Indeed the degree of catharsis employed by the artist would allow for a considerable distinction of terms. In a painting like 'There is no Night' by his son, Jack B. Yeats, a critic would rightly point to the degree of invention and fantasy separating the painting from any real landscape seen. In such a case the use of the word 'ecstasy' would help us to understand the mood of emotion to which Jack B. was possibly roused when invoking his 'There is no Night'. But the father was a portrait painter and he kept himself rigourously involved with his sitters. He was at pains therefore to give them accurate likeness as well as a certain flow of poetic invention to make the image truly a work of art. So he invokes the simpler term 'Dreamland' and reminds us of the emotions which exist between members of a loving family or people moved by grief or so on. He is always concerned in his writings with comparatively simple emotions and situations.

14

He was indeed a simple man fully aware that he could paint only that which he himself experienced.

> The other morning I woke out of my dreams, saying out loud several times over while still only half awake —
>
> "a man can only paint the life he has lived." [10]

It cannot be denied that JBY lived a life which engendered all kinds of imaginative ideas. He read deeply and talked so well that after his death in New York it was for his oratory and not for his painting that he was distinguished in obituary notices. It was however the quality of his mind which mainly accounted for his stature as an artist. First of all, he was an extraordinary failure. He failed to provide for himself or his family and he possibly had more financial success in his life-time as a writer and lecturer than in his chosen profession of portrait painter. Yet he nurtured all the elements of romance and idealism to keep away any quality of prosaic or vulgarising logic or practicality from the nature of his thoughts. 'But best of all I like the music, when the bird of poesy sings to itself in the heart of the wood, persuading and coaxing and commanding and admonishing its own soul, and thinking nothing of others' he wrote to WB.[11] No phrase seems better to suggest JBY than that. The idea of the bird of poesy admonishing its own soul and thinking nothing of others symbolises this portrait painter who began, every other day, another struggle to wrestle with his pen or brush and achieve that miracle which seemed always to be around the corner. He believed in the song which for him was the essential harmony in the portrait. Consequently he was prepared to struggle on in his solitary occupation. 'Art is solitary man, the man as he is behind the innermost, the utmost veils. That is why with the true poet we do not care what are his persuasions, opinions, ideas, religion, moralities — through all these we can pierce to the voice of the essential man if we have the discerning senses.' [12] And so he was always aware of his solitariness as an artist and he knew that no picture was finished if it did not, like the song, vibrate with a kind of music which brought balm to the viewer by its qualities of sympathy and tenderness.

As he so frequently wrote, JBY was concerned with an art which must contain a maximum of imagery and a maximum of music, words in fact which he applied to poetry because his main writings were addressed to his poet son though he was all the time writing from the standpoint of a painter. It is perfectly clear that he cultivated a habit of mind which would in every way direct his interests towards the creation of a peculiar portrait type. This portrait type we can identify in any of his main works, intensely humane, tender in the extreme and always suggesting the opposite of the aggressive, acquisitive, success-seeking man. In fact nearly all JBY's great portraits are of men and nearly all of them evoke idealistic, romantic and highly individual personalities. His own description of his fellow Irish as not representing the collective mind of the neighbouring Empire conveys better this idea.

> I have just been diligently reading in Turgeniev's memoirs of a sportsman — and have been impressed by the fact that the Russian peasant is like the Irishman — the Irishman of every kind and class, who is not west Briton. These men, Russian and Irish, are individualists, and interested only in individuals, in the poet, in the fighter, the lover, the witty talker, the man who sings, and indeed, in any strange fellow. I think it is a great matter for Ireland that she is a small island, and that she refuses to take any interest in the great affairs of the British Empire. She is like a child lost in a great Fair, who being

16

naughtily intrepid is not at all frightened, and on the contrary, delighted to be lost. Thus, we have escaped the collective mind, which for so many years has dulled the lustre of English life and tarnished the brightness of its poetry.[13]

II   THE HAND OF THE ARTIST

'Obviously a portrait painter is a craftsman — a born portrait painter as I believe myself to be (W. Osborne always said so) imprisoned in an imperfect technique — that has been my tragedy.'[14] In a sense JBY was apologising to his son WB when he wrote this in a letter in 1904. Like all true artists he was deeply dissatisfied with his technique and hoped for greater facility on every next day. What artist does not?

His earliest known works are drawings, in many cases delicate but slight studies capturing an attitude or a gesture or simply outlining a profile. Never have I seen one which suggests any hint of vulgarity or coarseness. This apparently was an attitude foreign to his kind of mind. Occasionally in his early drawings one notices tentativeness in lines which indicate the natural clumsiness of the inexperienced. Nevertheless every little pen and ink or pencil sketch contains the warmth of observation which was his abiding quality.

From the beginning he was captivated by the way in which people sat down or took up a position. He seemed to form a memory-image of pose and arrangement and then aimed to capture the general conception of character which this suggested. As far as the features were concerned he set himself the task of reflecting the mind of the sitter by making the eyes, nose and mouth suggest the thought being projected. For many years before taking up his profession he had learnt the art of

17

capturing facial resemblance and in general it could be said that for him this was never a problem. As he always aimed at inventing the mind behind the face, he was never easily pleased with a good outer resemblance. Sometimes he made sketches of people in parks or he drew landscapes with clever suggestiveness of masses of trees or areas of water. All of these were directed towards the revelation of forms in light. When on occasions he made fairly bold line drawings of elegant women's figures he still seemed to see them as forms dependent on the play of light from one or the other side. In the little pen or pencil drawings which would accompany notes or letters his ideas followed such a plan. He would, as it were, imagine the light flowing on the image and then hatch the shadows deepest on the opposite side. It is rare in the early work of artists not to be able to find a plain, tight, straight-forward outline drawing showing that the artist was trying to set up the outer shape of his subject as a basic structure in space.

In 1872 he received his first formal commission to paint the Herbert family of Muckross and a preliminary drawing (No. 8) remains in Senator Michael Yeats's Collection. Years later he was to meet members of the family in the U.S.A. who recalled to him their pleasure in these portraits.[15] From his early beginnings his affectionate, warm and sympathetic qualities, of course, gave pleasure, but always failed to find the approval which is so generally handed out to shallow and competent portrayers of what, from decade to decade, is regarded as fashionable, but is equally soon forgotten.

JBY was really a phenomenon in the way his work took on its own characteristics, reflecting nothing of the styles of Catterson Smith, Sarah Purser, Walter Osborne, or of his other contemporaries. To Osborne he was closest in sympathy, for Osborne was also deeply influenced by the fashionable impressionist technique of the day. Yet there is little resemblance between the two in actual technique since Osborne invariably set up an interior in which to place his figure whereas all JBY's sitters are conjured up from the background of paint on the canvas. He did share with Walter Osborne the respect for the theory that colour is a product of light rather than a constant value having an invariable tone. Thus in the works of both artists, touches of different colours were placed side by side to invoke the effect of flickering light on the clothes or skin.

It is interesting to read that JBY always considered himself to be an impressionist. In 1904 he came to regard himself as a competitor of the young Orpen, a brilliant artist of a far more academic character than JBY. After the exhibition of his works in the Gallery, 7 St. Stephen's Green, in 1901, Sir Hugh Lane had commissioned him to do a series of portraits of distinguished Irishmen. Lane later also commissioned Orpen to do a similar series and it is to this he refers in his letter of 1904 to WB:

> I have been painting Miss Lane in competition with Orpen, his style is learned like an old master, mine of course is modern and impressionist; however I am satisfied that mine is the better portrait. Orpen was most generous in his appreciation of my work. At least I thought I gathered this from conversation I overheard between him and Lane. He is of course exceedingly clever and very much in earnest. I heard him say to Miss Purser, "Do be serious — he has a great future".[16]

It was a measure of the simplicity of JBY and the sophistication of Orpen that he could take seriously such a remark from a man 40 years his junior.

The full-scale impressionist was marked by the pure colours of his palette and in particular the absence of black. JBY worked all his life with a great reliance on black, and though he frequently fused other colours into the surfaces of his darkest areas, he was by no stretch of the imagination a true impressionist. He was, however, deeply conscious of the importance of the effect of light and he rejected both in theory and practice the Orpen technique of contrasted surfaces which reconstituted the realism of furniture, draperies and china in a room as well as the elegant costume of the sitter placed therein. Indeed his abhorrence of such kinds of pictures was frequently stated and he attacked even such fashionable masters as Sargent whom he called a prose painter in contrast with Whistler, a poet painter.[17] The build-up of brilliant realistic surfaces in the work of Sargent presumably made him appear to JBY as more concerned with the recording of appearances than with the 'musical' rendering proper to a real 'songbird' like Whistler.

In order fully to appreciate the power of JBY's oil portraits it is necessary to observe that he invariably worked on the chosen image and built up the areas of flesh tone with touches of colour laid fresh on to the canvas within areas only faintly outlined in grey with strokes of the brush. This technique can indeed be discerned by the careful study of the canvas where the backgrounds are brushed in after the completion of the painting of the subject. In confirmation of this, the writer has several times had the good fortune to examine unfinished or partly painted works by JBY and to see the delicate build-up of pink, blue, orange, grey and other colours, all of which finally combine to create the required tones and textures which at a little distance set up the illusion of palpitating flesh in daylight. It was also something of a discovery to realise that a very small area of his brush-strokes create so instant and unmistakable an impression of his individual style that there is never any danger that his work will be confused with that of any other artist.

When he was living in 23 Fitzroy Road, London, he had a close friendship with three artists, Ellis, Nettleship, and Wilson. With them he formed a brotherhood and presumably out of this period came such paintings as 'Pippa Passes' and certain drawings, in particular the portrait of the artist's wife reproduced in William M. Murphy's study 'The Yeats Family and the Pollexfens of Sligo'. This study of Mrs. John Butler Yeats bears a striking resemblance to Ford Madox Brown's wife, Emma, in 'The Last of England' in the Birmingham Gallery, and altogether shows that for a brief interlude he dallied with the idea of the 'pre-raphaelite' mannerisms. Apart from these works he was consistently engaged from the beginning to the end of his life in his encounter with his private muse, whose demands apparently were only for greater facility of technique, not for alteration or development. The muse, however, to whom he had placed himself in lifelong subjection, demanded a fidelity to certain elements of goodness and sweetness that he might represent the men and women and children whom he portrayed as beings marked with a grace and intelligence which would reflect the singular character of their creator.

As in every poem he sought the poet, so in every picture he painted he hoped to reveal the noble characteristics of the painter. Once, writing for a life and selection of the letters of Frederick York Powell (Oxford, Clarendon Press 1906), he seemed to indicate this attitude of mind in the expression 'imaginative reason'. 'Meditation, experience of life, hope, charity, and all the emotions — out of these the imaginative reason speaks.'

It seems then, that though he struggled with the physical

problems of painting, he was always rather more involved with the psychological problem of conveying the spirit of his sitters. He wrote one letter from New York to his son WB which is such a perfect example of the nature of his mind, his concern for the plight of individuals and his involvement with them that I feel it is necessary to quote it in full.

My dear Willie — People do not understand the importance, the significance of exact portraiture in art. In every picture, in every poem, there must be somewhere an exact portraiture — otherwise there is no work of art.

Two summers ago, one day at mid-noon, when the strong sun had killed all the breezes, I was taking my daily walk without which I have no health, keeping on the west side as close to the Hudson, as possible, the water being refreshing to look at, and it being a place where gathered few people (in hot weather to see other people as hot as oneself always adds to my distress), when quite suddenly I came on an open space with little gardens and all crowded with children. As these were all quite happy and careless of the heat and as I was curious to see what brought them, naturally I stopped and mingled among them. I looked about for an elder person whom I might question. Close to me stood a young woman, and when she answered my questions I knew by her voice that she was Irish, and to my surprise I found she was from Donnybrook. She was also very pretty, with a gentle sad-eyed expression, such as one seldom finds in New York. I then noticed that she held a baby in her arms, and that when I glanced toward it she tried to conceal it from me with her hand. It was asleep, but wasted and scrofulous and very sick, its arms and legs so thin that the hands and feet looked large; in its

22

wasted neck there were lumps. I could not resist ques-
tioning her and found that she had had two other children
who died in infancy and that her father and mother in
Ireland were dead and that she did not expect to go there
again, and that her husband was a healthy man, etc. etc.
She spoke with resignation as if to the will of God, or
Fate — I did not know which. She spoke of the child's
sickness as being due to teething, as if she wished to think
it temporary. As a contrast all around were swarms of
healthy children, obstreperous and noisy. She looked at
them as if she did not see them.

I came away, and for days and weeks almost to this
hour I am haunted and oppressed by the feeling of grief,
of poignant depression which suddenly assailed me as
I talked to that poor young woman. Had I been an active-
minded philanthropist or a suffragette indignant with a
man-managed world, I'd have got busy and never rested
till I eased my heart by doing something to help. As to
myself I felt as helpless as would have been a mediaeval
artist — even though I was not prepared to say that such
suffering was punishment inflicted by a just God — and
being as helpless as one of these my mental process was
probably the same as theirs. Why did I look at her so
constantly, not being able to take away my eyes, and
why did I ask so many questions , such as perhaps would
have been resented by a woman less gentle and good?
(perhaps also being Irish she thought she owed respect
to one so much older), and why did I, after I left her
hoping in a cowardly way never to see her again, make
every effort of memory to recall every detail of what
I said and of what she told me? The answer is that every
feeling and especially it might seem the painful feeling,
tries to keep itself alive, and not only that but to increase

in strength. This is the law of human nature and is what I have called the spirit of growth — in other words, I would have given worlds to have painted a careful study of her and her sick infant and carried it away with me to keep my sorrow alive. Here we have art as portraiture, a kind of art great in its way; there is also the conflict of feelings — the ghastly repulsive sickness of the infant, the real charm of the mother's face and form, her mother pride all abashed, her hopelessness and yet her effort to be hopeful that it was only teething. This hopefulness, itself a conscious lie, said perhaps out of a social instinct to ease the situation as she talked to me, and then her manifest love as she looked down at the child asleep, blissfully sleeping. Of course such portraiture is incomplete art — so the artists and poets of old invented the Madonna with the divine infant. But in this case and in these times there is no Madonna with the divine infant, and the artist, having made his portrait, must pass by on his way, unless indeed he pays a visit to the Philanthropists — and in this particular case they could do nothing. The artist would be excused if he threw a little touch of rhetoric into his portraiture, such as the crowd loves — though if philanthropists were cultivated as well as rich, they would only offend and bring his truthfulness into doubt, convicting him of vulgarity and commonness.

At any rate have I not made it obvious that all art begins in portraiture? That is, a realistic thing identified with realistic feeling, after which and because of which comes the Edifice of Beauty — the great reaction. — Yours affectionately — J. B. Yeats.

I think I have already written to you that it is ugliness which created beauty. The purely beautiful only breeds weariness or rather laziness — vacuity.[18]

JBY here identified portraiture with the realistic feeling to be found in life's actuality. As he said he longed to paint a careful study of the girl and her sick infant to keep his sorrow alive. To this careful study he would have to add the Edifice of Beauty. On another occasion he spoke of beauty as the lovable made visible and added that beauty was also wondrous, magnetic and astonishing.[19]

In his great series of portraits commencing perhaps with Isaac Butt (N.G.I. 2442) and including John O'Leary (N.G.I. 869), Hyde (N.G.I. 874), Moore (N.G.I. 873), O'Grady (N.G.I. 870), and many other distinguished figures of Irish history as well as all the members of his own family, he has succeeded in showing the most diverse and individual of characters with an extraordinary sense of dignity and unifying style. I suspect that he rarely drew or painted any of them without coming to regard them with affection and goodwill. This he always conveys. He never hesitates to accentuate individual character-istics, the astringent reticence of Moore, the pedantic intensity of Katharine Tynan Hinkson, the bland and uninspired genial-ity of Hyde; all these ideas are well conveyed but nowhere with any hint of astringency or in any way suggesting a caustic approach.

The greatest artists of portraiture, Titian, Rembrandt, Van Dyck, Hogarth, Lawrence, all were marked by a profound respect for the values we call humanitarian in their sitters. They went even further and showed a reverence for the pathos of human weakness and frailty. It seems to me that JBY shared these attributes with the great masters and, like them, communicated his sympathy in a unique and remark-able technique. All artists of true sensibility are likewise marked by the originality of their style, and JBY is a shining example of a stylist who cannot be compared with any of his contemporaries. He is closest in affinity with painters like

Corot or Courbet for the delicate way he builds up the structure of the figure and keeps it subject to the imaginative requirements of the personality. But in actual surface technique he is uniquely his own man, employing his brush strokes and colours to bring before us a whole range of late 19th and 20th century figures distinguished either on the Irish national or political field. By his delicate tones and by working from a ground of indeterminate colour he sets up a space proper only to the spiritual environment of his sitter. The features, the concept of breathing and movement are then somehow invoked until we feel ourselves able to examine the portrait through the elements of paint and then to forget the paint and to find the personality. This sensitivity to surface qualities is a mark of the work of Venetian painters of the 16th century as of 17th century masters everywhere. The great masters of Impressionism once again brought the method to the fore and though one can hardly place JBY amongst his French contemporaries, one can nevertheless see that he devised a style for himself here in Ireland which is extremely similar in many respects. Since, however, he was united with a world of literature deeply invigorated by an underlying resurgence towards a concept of nationhood which made the writers and artists of the time vibrant with passionate conviction and ideas, he was inspired to use a more vaporous surface than his French contemporaries.

In 1910 his patron and friend, John Quinn, impressed with JBY's portraits of John O'Leary at an exhibition of 'Independents' in New York, gave him a sort of dream commission. He invited him to paint a large self-portrait — to take his time and name his own price. He worked on this picture intermittently for the rest of his life and he described it as 'myself seen through a glass darkly' (see frontispiece). He frequently wrote about this work and felt it would be regarded as his magnum opus. He told Quinn in a letter dated 1919.

> Whenever a Petitpas approaches I see in her manner a
> stealthy menace, and I should be frightfully worried but
> for one thing — the portrait. I am delighted with it. It
> is like watching a blessed ghost of a long lost beloved
> slowly materialising. I think of nothing else and I dream
> of it. My bitter hours are now only notes. When you get
> it and it is hung on your walls, it will have a stark reality
> that will outweigh all the other portraits, even John's
> Portrait of you. At least that is how it now seems to me,
> just now immediately after breakfast which with me is
> always a time of good hope, which, however often fades
> away in the evening.[20]

This great portrait is covered with heavy impasto and tingles
with myriad little touches of colour invoking all the modern
artists collected by John Quinn. It retains exactly JBY's old
style of conjuring up the figure with paint from its own base
rather than as a form isolated in an interior. Nevertheless he
made an interior and shows light pouring in from the left
and piles of books on a mantleshelf behind, as well as a collection of painting-pots in the foreground. He does realise
space as he never before has done but at the same time all his
textures and tones create a uniformity which gives the work
the traditional JBY touch. It is a masterpiece of modern
portraiture by a man who was over 60 before the year 1900.

It is heartening to be able to study his last self-portrait and
to reflect that all his life-long ambitions were realised. He did
end up a truly avant garde painter, technically as well as in
subject matter. Even today in Ireland to where the self-portrait
has come (Coll. Senator Yeats) it is not appreciated or under-
stood as it deserves. But the position of JBY is secure, and

27

having survived that valley period after death when reputations sometimes sink, he now takes his place as the most sensitive portrait painter in this country.

He died on 2 February 1922, in New York. That fine American painter, John Sloan, whose oil painting 'Yeats in Petitpas', showing JBY amongst his American friends, hangs in the Corcoran Art Gallery in Washington, wrote to JBY's daughter what should be regarded by any artist as a fitting epitaph:

My dear Miss Yeats — That great man your father is no longer with us; we expected him to go — not the mysterious journey into the great beyond — we expected him to go home to Ireland but we had an unformed hope that he would never go. He has gone, gone easily with serenity and for me the world can never be the same — the great warm glow has gone. But I should have felt about the same had he left for Ireland. He would then have been with you and not with us — now he is with us all.

His was a swift illness — hardly an illness — confined to his room one day, to his bed one day and then away to take first rank among the mighty poets of the past.

We did love him and he loved us. We have the usual regrets — feel that we did not see him enough — appreciate him enough, I think these are the common regrets, moments of realization of how selfish is each part played in the farce of life — some day we may play the drama, I believe that will be nobler.

Let your sister and brothers know how deeply I sympathise with you all.

The Church from which he was buried was full of his lovers, about 250 people there (with only 24 hours notice) and they each felt as I did, that they had lost their father — I assure you that my own father's death was not so great a loss to me. I was never as near to him as to John Butler Yeats, we did not understand each other — and had the Puritan standoffishness — no love expressed, all repression.

A few score men such as your father in the world at any one time would cure its sickness — but our civilization produces other flowers — unsavoury blooms rank and poisonous — John Butler Yeats was one of the rare exceptions. — With etc. — (Signed) John Sloan.[21]

NOTES

Quotations from : *J. B. Yeats. Letters to his Son, W. B. Yeats & Others, 1869–1922*, edited by Joseph Hone, London, Faber & Faber, 1944.

1	Memoir	*page 25*	12	Letter No. 132	p. 193
2	Letter No. 2	p. 48	13	Letter No. 184	p. 239
3	Letter No. 121	p. 179	14	Letter No. 39	p. 79
4	Letter No. 69	p. 121	15	Letter No. 169	p. 230
5	Letter No. 126	p. 185	16	Letter No. 35	p. 75
6	Letter No. 93	p. 147	17	Letter No. 56	p. 102
7	Letter No. 233	pp. 275/6	18	Letter No. 131	pp. 191/2
8	Letter No. 82	p. 136	19	Letter No. 113	p. 170
9	Letter No. 136	pp. 198/9	20	Letter No. 210	p. 260
10	Letter No. 47	p. 93	21	Letter No. 251	p. 289
11	Letter No. 111	p. 168			

JEANNE ROBERT FOSTER

JOHN BUTLER YEATS

("*Alas, for the wonderful yew forest!*")

We shall remember him
As a man who had a little in him of the men of all time.
We shall remember him —
This tall, lean-shouldered, witty Irishman,
Master of the art of conversation,
Jesting with us in his high-pitched Irish voice,
That lilted to a delicate string
Beyond our hearing.
"Shakespeare was a kindly man," he often said.
John Yeats was a kindly man
Who gave lavishly of himself
As if life had no end.
Around him gathered
The tangible aroma of life
Full-flavoured with intense living.
"Ireland is kind," he said.
"She has many faults, but I feel about her
As I do about Heaven.
If Heaven were a perfect place it would bore me.
I like to think of Heaven as a place with discords;
As a beautiful orchestration with Love as master of the music."
"Montaigne said" — that phrase was often on his lips.
Stories of wits and poets and artists,
Memories of Morris and Samuel Butler and Dowden,
Brilliant débris of irrecoverable personality.
"The artist is the only happy man," he told us.

31

"Art springs from a mood of divine unreason.
Unreason is when a man cannot be at peace with eternal
     conditions."
We shall remember him intimately
As we knew him — his room, his pipes, his drawings.
We shall remember him sitting at his easel,
Keen-eyed, young, eager to live a thousand years,
Unwearied by life,
Sheltered beneath the green tree of his own thoughts.
We shall remember him
Ripening like an apple in quiet sunshine.
Responsive to human affection,
And — patient of our human limitations —
Writing, under his own portrait
(Painted from his reflection in a mirror),
"Myself seen through a glass darkly."

Printed in *The New York Times*, 6 February 1922

DRAMATIS PERSONÆ

The cover is derived from a self-portrait
made in 1905, also printed opposite

33

FAMILY

WILLIAM BUTLER YEATS, 1865–1939 :
The first-born of the union of JBY and Susan Pollexfen, he seems to have resisted formal education to some extent. He went to the High School, Dublin, and later to the Metropolitan College of Art, Dublin, to study painting. He read privately in Trinity College and elsewhere and first published his poems in the *Dublin University Review* in 1885. His poems were also read aloud at the Contemporary Club and voted on by the members when he was only twenty. 'Young Yeats is the only person in this room who will ever be reckoned a genius' O'Leary prophesised in the Club. (*John O'Leary* by Marcus Bourke, Anvil Books Ltd., Tralee.)

All his life JBY acted as a spur to his son W. B., endeavouring to make him the creator of songs and lyrics rather than the man of the theatre which JBY attributed to Lady Gregory's influence.

MRS. JOHN BUTLER YEATS
(née Susan Pollexfen), 1841–1900 :
Daughter of William Pollexfen, merchant and shipowner in the town of Sligo, and Elizabeth Midleton, daughter of a wealthy Sligo shipowner already related to the Pollexfens.

In 1863 she married John Butler Yeats, a close personal friend of her brother, George Pollexfen. There were 6 children of the union : the poet W. B., Robert, who died at the age of 3, Jack B. the painter, Lily (Susan Mary), Lollie (Elizabeth) and Jane Grace, who survived less than a year. Mrs. Yeats had a difficult life due to the failure of her husband to make satisfactory income and she suffered much bad health resulting in a stroke in 1887. She died on 3 January 1900 after an illness lasting 12 years. See William M. Murphy's *The Yeats Family and The Pollexfens of Sligo* published by The Dolmen Press.

MRS. W. B. YEATS, 1895–1968 :
Georgie Hyde-Lees was born in England on 17 October 1895, daughter of William Gilbert Hyde-Lees. Her mother married a second time and it was with her brother's sister, Olivia Shakespeare, that she first met W. B. Yeats, whom she subsequently married in 1917.

She had marked musical and literary interests and was always of great assistance to her husband, apart from also sharing his interests in the occult.

At first they lived in London but as WBY wished his first child to be born in Ireland they settled in Dublin and later took a cottage attached to Ballylee Castle into which they ultimately moved. They had two children : Anne, the artist, and Michael, Chairman of the Irish Senate.

She survived her husband for many years and also assisted in keeping the Cuala Press going.

2 Mrs. John Butler Yeats

3   William Butler Yeats   4   Mrs. W. B. Yeats *opposite*

LILY YEATS, 1866–1949 :
Born at Enniscrone, near Sligo, and christened Susan Mary. She was the eldest of the daughters of JBY. She studied embroidery under May Morris, who was later her assistant. She also worked for Dun Emer Guild. She and her sister, Lollie, took a house in Dundrum for themselves and their father, which they called Gurteen Dhas. At this time she and her father used to walk in to Dublin city, a distance of about five miles. 'But,' according to Joseph Hone, 'they never walked together, for they could not agree as to which was the shorter road. The father always arrived first, but it was suspected that he ran for part of the way.'

LOLLIE YEATS, 1868–1940 :
Born at 23 Fitzroy Road, London, and christened Elizabeth Corbet, she was the second daughter of JBY. She worked as a teacher of Art in a London County Council School. She studied the hand press at the same time as her sister Lily was working at embroidery with May Morris. It was Lollie who was largely responsible for the production of the broad sheets of Jack B. Yeats in The Cuala Industries. In forty years the Cuala Press published over sixty books from a hand press. JBY wrote that she would have carved out a path of her own choosing had she had a father capable of making a decent living.

JACK B. YEATS, 1871–1957 :
Born in London, 29 August 1871, the fifth child of JBY. From 1879–1887 he lived with his Pollexfen grandparents in Sligo and then attended art schools in London : (1) South Kensington; (2) Chiswick Art School; (3) Westminster School. He worked as a black and white illustrator with some success. He had his first one-man show at the Clifford Gallery, London, in 1897. He exhibited drawings, watercolours and oil paintings variously and continuously in Ireland, England, France and America until his death in 1957. See Thomas MacGreevy *Jack B. Yeats*, Victor Waddington, Dublin 1948. Hilary Pyle *Jack B. Yeats*, a biography, Routledge & Kegan Paul 1970. James White (with Hilary Pyle) *Jack B. Yeats Drawings and Paintings*, Secker & Warburg, London 1971.

GEORGE POLLEXFEN, 1839–1910 :
Son of William Pollexfen, shipowner and miller in Sligo town, he attended the Atholl Academy in the Isle of Man with his two brothers and the three Yeats brothers, of whom JBY was his special friend. He entertained the boys at night with his stories, and had a quality of magnetism which he only revealed in private, according to JBY. It was while visiting him that JBY met his future wife, George's sister, Susan. He was an excellent jockey and an expert in the study of astrology. Both W. B. and Jack B. likewise were conscious of their Uncle George Pollexfen's magnetism.

38

6 Elizabeth Corbet (Lollie) Yeats
opposite

7 Jack B. Yeats

8 George Pollexfen

FORERUNNERS

JOHN O'LEARY, 1830–1907:
Born 23 July 1830 in Tipperary. Educated at Tipperary Grammar School, Carlow College, Trinity College, Dublin, Queens College, Cork, Queens College, Galway, where he pursued medicine but did not finally qualify.

In 1855 he went to Paris and made a friendship which lasted all his life with James A. McN. Whistler, the famous American painter. He, Whistler, Swinburne the poet, and J. E. Poynter, P.R.H.A., the English painter, shared lodgings in Paris for a year. George de Maurier was also one of the fraternity.

He became acquainted with James Stephens and the Fenian movement and was later Editor of the *Irish People*, the official organ of the I.R.B. The paper was seized by the government in 1863 and O'Leary tried for treason and felony, and on 6 February 1864 he was sentenced to twenty years penal servitude. He was released in 1870 and returned to Ireland in 1885. In 1896 he published his *Recollections of Fenians and Fenianism*.

At his house in Terenure he kept a literary salon where he entertained a group including Douglas Hyde, Rolleston, A.E., Stephen Gwynn, William Stokley, JBY and W. B. Yeats. 'Here he urged ceaselessly his talented disciples to try their hands at writing prose and poetry with a national content, without which he believed no political revolution in Ireland would bring lasting results.'

See *John O'Leary* by Marcus Bourke, Anvil Books Ltd., Tralee.

STANDISH O'GRADY, 1846–1915:
Born in 1846 at Castletown Berehaven, Co. Cork, where his father was Church of Ireland rector. In 1868 he graduated from Trinity College, Dublin, and was called to the Bar where he practiced for some time, later taking up journalism. He became well known as a writer of prose and poetry. He edited *The Kilkenny Review* and later founded and edited the *All Ireland Review*.

Amongst his publications was *The History of Ireland : Heroic Period* (1878; 2 vols.). See bibliography of S. J. O'Grady by P. S. O'Hegarty in the *Dublin Magazine*, Vol. 5, No. 2 (April 1930).

overleaf
9   John O'Leary
10   Standish O'Grady

11 William Morris
12 Alfred Percival Graves

WILLIAM MORRIS, 1834–1896 :
Educated at Exeter College, Oxford, with Burne-Jones, Morris evolved and carried out his own theory of socialist and productive art. He found a practical outlet in his Kelmscott Press, and through his own total designs. JBY read the poetry of Morris to his children, and 'The Yeatses house, 8 Woodstock Rd., had a bathroom, and Morris paper on the walls' (Joseph Hone, *W. B. Yeats*).

In *John O'Leary* by Marcus Bourke, it is stated that at the Contemporary Club 'visitors were frequently introduced, amongst the earliest was the famous artist, poet and socialist, William Morris.'

ALFRED PERCIVAL GRAVES, 1846–1931:
Author and educationalist. Educated at Windermere College and Trinity College, Dublin. Inspector of schools at Manchester, Huddersfield and Taunton, publishing *Songs of old Ireland* (including 'Father O'Flynn'), and *Songs of Erin* (1892), in collaboration with C. V. Stanford. From 1895 he worked in London, (the Celtic Psaltery was published in 1917) contributing to *Punch* and taking a leading part in the newly formed London Irish Literary Society. He returned to Wales and there produced, in reply to the autobiography of his son Robert, his own autobiography *To return to all that.*

46

LADY ISABELLE AUGUSTA GREGORY, 1852–1932 :
Born 1852, Roxborough, Co. Galway. Daughter of Dudley Persse. In 1880 she married Sir William Gregory of Coole Park. He was 63 and she 28. They travelled widely, but her main interest was folklore and Irish literature. She joined the Gaelic League and went to Aran to learn Irish. She published *Cuchulann of Muirthemne*, the stories of the gods and fighting men of Ireland, in 1902.

1897 at Coole Park, Edward Martyn brought W. B. Yeats to visit Lady Gregory and it was as a result of this first meeting that the new Irish theatre was born. *The Countess Cathleen* by W. B. Yeats was produced by the Irish Literary Theatre and in 1904 the Abbey Theatre was opened, the directors being W. B. Yeats, Synge and Lady Gregory. After Lady Gregory's death, W. B. Yeats said of her : 'She has been to me mother, friend, sister and brother. I cannot realise the world without her — she brought to my wavering thoughts steadfast nobility.' JBY felt keenly this influence which Lady Gregory exerted on his poet son and once wrote to him : 'Had you stayed with me and not left me for Lady Gregory, and her friends and associations you would have loved and adored concrete life for which as I know you have a real affection'. (Letter 229, *J. B. Yeats. Letters to his Son W. B. Yeats and Others.*)

13 Lady Gregory

SIR HUGH PERCY LANE, 1875–1915 :
Born 1875, Ballybrack, Co. Cork. Travelled widely in boyhood and was taught
some picture restoring when he was about
16. He worked for Martin Colnaghi at
the Marlborough Gallery, London, and
opened his own gallery at 2 Pall Mall
Place in 1898. In 1900 he met W. B.
Yeats and other Irish writers in Coole
with his aunt, Lady Gregory. He visited
the exhibition of the paintings of
Nathaniel Hone and JBY at The Gallery,
6 St. Stephen's Green, in 1901 and was
deeply impressed. He then commissioned
JBY to paint a series of portraits of
famous figures in Irish life for the benefit
of the gallery he was then creating
for Ireland. In 1902 he organised an
exhibition of Old Masters in Dublin and
in 1904 of Irish artists in the Guildhall,
London. He exhibited works from the
Staats Forbes Collection in Dublin in
1905, and in 1908 opened the Munipical
Gallery of Modern Art in Harcourt St.,
and presented to it 154 works of art.
When a new building as specified by him
was not agreed on, in 1913 he withdrew
39 pictures and gave them to the National
Gallery, London. He subsequently made
a codicil to his will, which was not
witnessed, stating his wish that these
pictures should after all be given to
Dublin as he originally intended. The
considerable controversy arising is fully
dealt with in Lady Gregory's *Sir Hugh
Lane*, a new edition of which will shortly
be published by Colin Smythe, Gerrards
Cross, London. See also Thomas Bodkin
Hugh Lane and his Pictures (Dublin
Stationery Office).

14   Sir Hugh Percy Lane

49

EDWARD MARTYN, 1859–1923 :
Born 1859. Educated at Belvedere College,
Dublin, Beaumont, and Christ Church,
Oxford. He lived in Co. Galway and was
a man of wide political and cultural
interests. He founded the co-operative
stained glass firm *An Tur Gloine* and the
Palestrina Choir in the Pro-Cathedral
Dublin. He was a member and President
of Sinn Fein and author of *The Heather
Field*, *Maeve*, and other plays. There is a
long and brilliant portrait of him by
George Moore in his autobiography *Hail
and Farewell*.

KATHARINE TYNAN HINKSON,
1861–1931 :
Born 1861, in Clondalkin, Co. Dublin,
and educated at the Dominican Convent,
Drogheda. A novelist and poetess of
distinction including *Twenty Five Years*
and *The Middle Years*. She married in
1893 an Irish R.M. and novelist, Henry
A. Hinkson. It was in the house of her
father, Andrew Cullen Tynan, that JBY
met a large circle of Irish literary people.
JBY accused Protestant Dublin of being
very ungracious towards so sweet a young
poetess as Katharine Tynan, according to
Joseph Hone's Memoir in *J. B. Yeats.
Letters to his Son W. B. Yeats and Others*.

15   Edward Martyn

50

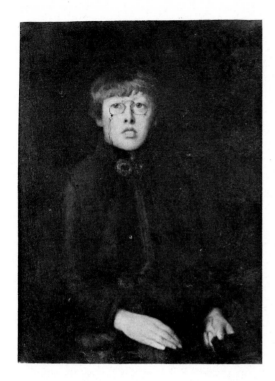

GEORGE MOORE, 1852–1933 :

Born 1852, Co. Mayo. Educated at Oscott College. Studied art for a short time at the Academie Julian in Paris. Later he came to know Manet, Monet, Degas, Pissaro and other prominent painters and wrote some art criticism. He was a fine novelist, author of *Esther Waters* and other works and renowned for his trilogy *Hail and Farewell*. He assisted Martyn and W. B. Yeats in the foundation of the Irish Literary Theatre. Once, describing a visit in a letter to his son WB, JBY wrote : 'How volcanic the ground always is at Moore's. What a pity if the sullen peace of a mutual distrust should settle over the scene.' On another occasion he said it was as bad to be a poet's father as the intimate friend of George Moore.

DR. DOUGLAS HYDE, 1860–1949 :

Born Frenchpark, Co. Roscommon. Son of a clergyman. Educated at home, learning Irish orally from local native speakers. Entered TCD 1880. A great linguist, knowing Latin, Greek, Hebrew, French, German, Irish and English. Studied theology and later law. He devoted himself to writing, collecting and translating Irish literature and preserving the language. His work was an inspiration to many writers including Yeats. 1893 first President of the Gaelic League, which had 550 branches by 1905. Unsuccessfully tried to keep the League non-political and non-sectarian, resigning 1915. 1908–1932 Professor of Modern Irish in UCD; 1925 and 1937, Senator; 1937–1945, first President of Ireland.

When *The Tinker and the Fairy*, written by him, was performed in George Moore's garden at Ely Place in the summer of 1902, the part of the Tinker was played by Douglas Hyde and that of the Fairy was played by Miss Flanagan, now Mrs. De Valera, wife of Ireland's President at the time of writing.

16 Katharine Tynan Hinkson

17   George Moore

18 Douglas Hyde

GEORGE WILLIAM RUSSELL (AE),
1867–1935 :
Born Lurgan, Co. Armagh. Educated
Model School, Lurgan; Art School, Kildare
Street, and Dr. Benson's, Rathmines.
Studied at the Metropolitan School of Art,
where he met W. B. Yeats and through
whom he became interested in theosophy.
He worked as a clerk and published
Homeward : Songs by the Way in 1894.
In 1897 he joined the Irish Agricultural
Organisation Society and made its pub-
lication, *Irish Homestead*, a popular and
interesting journal. He wrote on mystic-
ism, and was a great conversationalist.

JBY wrote that 'AE would cure all the
ills of Ireland by setting up a priesthood
and a church and be as anxious for the
material prosperity of his devotees as
other churches are, and for the same
reason. Liberation has no value for him
except as a mystical doctrine.'

See *Letters from AE* edited by Alan
Denson, Abelard-Schuman, which contains a bibliography.

CONSTANCE de MARCIEVICZ,
1868–1927 :
Born 1868. Eldest daughter of Sir Henry
Gore-Booth, Bart., of Lissadell, Sligo.
Married in 1900 Casimir Dunin, Count de
Marcievicz (of Staro Zyvotov, Poland)
a painter.

She studied painting in Paris but became absorbed in the struggle for Irish
freedom. She helped James Connolly
during the strike of 1913, and in the
Rising was second in command at the
Royal College of Surgeons.

Received into the Catholic Church in
1916, and was condemned to death after
the Rising. Her death sentence was com-
muted to penal servitude for life; released
1917, after which she continued to take
a prominent part in political life. She was
the first woman to be elected to the
House of Commons though she never
took her seat.

Madame Marchevitz

55

PADRAIC COLUM, 1881–1971 :
Born at Longford in 1881. His father went
to America, the only man to cross the
Atlantic and unable to find work, according to his poet son. Employed early
as a railway clerk. He published *The
Children of Lir* when he was 18. In 1912
he married the critic Mary Catherine
Maguire and they emigrated to America
where he obtained lectureships and assistance with his publications. He dedicated
his first collection of Poems *Wild Earth*
to 'AE who fostered me'. As well as
many other books of poems he wrote a
biography of Arthur Griffith and in collaboration with his wife *Our friend James
Joyce*.

He was a close friend of JBY and they
had planned together, in New York, to
paint Dublin red when they returned.
Padraic, of course, visited Dublin frequently but JBY never left New York.

JOHN MILLINGTON SYNGE, 1871–1909 :
Born Newtown Little near Rathfarnham.
Educated at Trinity College, Dublin, and
RIAM. Lived in Paris from 1895, until
his fateful meeting in 1899 with W. B.
Yeats. He acted on Yeats's suggestion
that he should go to the Aran Islands
and find a life that had never been
expressed in literature, instead of a life
where all had been expressed. Stories
from the Aran Islands suggested the plots
of his first plays *The Shadow of the Glen*
(produced, 1903) and *Riders to the Sea*
(produced, 1904). One of three literary
advisors to the Abbey Theatre, 1904,
where his most famous play *The Playboy
of the Western World* was produced in
1907.

Deirdre of The Sorrows was left unfinished at his death. When W. B. Yeats
received the Nobel Prize he commented
that J. M. Synge and Lady Gregory should
be standing by, one on either side.

22　John Millington Synge

23 John Eglinton

JOHN EGLINTON, 1868–1961 :
William Kirkpatrick Magee, born 1868
in Dublin, wrote under the pseudonym
'John Eglinton'. With Frederick Ryan
edited *Dana*. His books include *Pebbles
from a Brook*, *Irish Literary Portraits*, a
memoir of AE, a selection from Edward
Dowden's letters and a selection of letters
written to him by George Moore. His
father was Presbyterian Minister and John
Eglinton worked on the staff of The
National Library in Dublin for many
years.

JBY wrote : 'I think Magee with all
his abilities is a prominent member of
the farm yard — since to this trick of
criticism he adds an admiration for the
fait accompli which makes him turn
eyes of admiration so constantly on
things English.' W. B. Yeats called AE's
circle of young poets 'AE's Farmyard'.

SUSAN MITCHELL, 1886–1926 :
Susan Langstaff Mitchell was born in
Carrick-on-Shannon where her father was
a bank manager. She lived for a time with
JBY's family at Bedford Park in London
and later in Sligo and Dublin. She worked
as sub-editor of *The Irish Homestead* and
subsequently *The Irish Statesman*.

She was a poetess who published widely
and was greatly admired by AE and JBY,
who wrote of her constantly with admiration. He noted she had a quality of
intensity missing from AE and WBY.
'If you would write more and use your
own life more, we should not only have
more poetry, but it would be stronger
and more intimate.' (*J. B. Yeats. Letters
to his Son W. B. Yeats and Others.*)

KUNO MEYER, 1858–1919 :
Educated in Germany, England, Scotland
and Ireland. Introduced research into early
Irish MSS., publishing *Grammatica Celtica*
in 1853, and the Irish version of the
Alexander Legend in 1884. Returned to
Germany to take the chair of Celtic
Philology in Berlin, producing numerous
treatises in his subject. When JBY re-
turned to Ireland they became close
friends but when Kuno Meyer was in
America seeking Irish sympathies for
Germany in 1916, JBY refused to see
him saying that he could not forget the
Lusitania — it was between them as a
skeleton out of cupboards. (Letter 153.
*John Butler Yeats. Letters to his Son W. B.
Yeats and Others.*)

ERNEST A. BOYD, 1887–1946 :
In his *Ireland's Literary Renaissance*
Ernest Boyd tells of the Theosophic
Movement originating 'one afternoon at
Dowden's house, when W. B. Yeats was
present, somebody spoke of a strange
book which had just appeared — A. P.
Sinnett's *Esoteric Buddhism*'. In the same
work he quotes Yeats as saying that
Russell and the Theosophists on the one
hand, and Standish O'Grady on the other,
had done more for Irish literature than
Trinity College in the course of three
centuries.

He joined the exiles of the 'canary-
bird' period, to review his old hero-
worship of W.B. in America. He recalled
that the aged poet even went so far as
to recite 'The Salley Gardens' — 'one of
his early poems he had at one time been
wont to belittle' (Joseph Hone, *W. B.
Yeats*, Macmillan & Co. Ltd. London).

26 Ernest Boyd

61

THEATRE

27   Annie F. Horniman

ANNIE F. HORNIMAN, 1860-1937:
Born 1860. Studied painting at the Slade under Legros. Helped finance performances of *The Land of Heart's Desire* and Shaw's *Arms and the Man*, at the Avenue Theatre, London, during 1894. 'Her interest in the theatre and in Yeats brought her to Dublin in 1903, where she designed and made the costumes for Yeats's *The King's Threshold*.

It was through the generosity of Miss Horniman that the Irish National Theatre Company acquired the Abbey Theatre in 1904. Her connection with the Abbey — and her annual subsidy — endured until 1911.

JBY's portrait of her in the Abbey Theatre records a most sensitive personality and is a permanent record of her generosity to that theatre.

FRANK FAY, 1870–1931:
Born 1870, Dublin, elder brother of William G. Fay. Educated at Marlborough Street School.

One of the founders of the Irish National Theatre Company. Had a long stage career in the U.S. and in England, retiring with his family to Dublin where he taught elocution.

62

28   Frank Fay

29   W. G. Fay

30   Maire Nic Shiubhlaigh

31   J. M. Kerrigan

WILLIAM G. FAY, 1872–1947 :
Born 1872, Dublin ; educated at Belvedere College. A noted actor and theatre manager, he played in Ireland, England and the United States.

In 1903, in conjunction with Lady Gregory, George Russell and W. B. Yeats inaugurated the Irish National Theatre Company; in 1904 took up the management of the Abbey Theatre. Resigned — following disagreement on policy with directors — 1908. Had a long stage career, like his elder brother, Frank, in the U.S. and in England.

MAIRE NIC SHIUBHLAIGH, 1883–1950 :
Distinguished Abbey actress. When Miss Horniman proposed in 1905 to pay the players salaries, there were disadvantages as well as advantages. ' . . . it turned the Theatre from an enterprise undertaken for love of Ireland and dramatic art into a "commercial" theatre. It was not unnatural that a split should result and (with others) Maire Nic Shiubhlaigh resigned.'

J. M. KERRIGAN, 1885–1964 :
Born 1885, Dublin. Educated at Belvedere College, Dublin. As an Abbey actor he played in Ireland, England and the United States. JBY painted a portrait of him in New York.

W. B. YEATS

BEAUTIFUL LOFTY THINGS

Beautiful lofty things : O'Leary's noble head;
My father upon the Abbey stage, before him a raging crowd :
'This Land of Saints,' and then as the applause died out,
'Of plaster Saints'; his beautiful mischievous head thrown
    back.
Standish O'Grady supporting himself between the tables
Speaking to a drunken audience high nonsensical words;
Augusta Gregory seated at her great ormolu table,
Her eightieth winter approaching : 'Yesterday he threatened
    my life.
I told him that nightly from six to seven I sat at this table,
The blinds drawn up'; Maud Gonne at Howth station waiting
    a train,
Pallas Athene in that straight back and arrogant head :
All the Olympians; a thing never known again.

From New Poems, *The Cuala Press Dublin 1938. Reprinted by permission of Miss Anne Yeats and Senator Michael B. Yeats.*

PAINTINGS AND DRAWINGS BY JOHN BUTLER YEATS FROM THE COLLECTION OF SENATOR MICHAEL B. YEATS AND THE NATIONAL GALLERY OF IRELAND

Shown at the National Gallery of Ireland from 30 November 1972 to mark the fiftieth anniversary of the artist's death

All drawings and pictures are from the Collection of Senator Michael Yeats except those marked with an asterisk (*), which are from the Collection of the National Gallery of Ireland or have been deposited there by the Municipal Gallery of Modern Art, Dublin.

Abbreviations: wc: watercolour   s: signed   d: dated   insc: inscribed

	DRAWINGS	Size (cms)
1	Old couple and girl in park	38.0 × 50.5
2*	Pippa Passes wc	48.0 × 34.0
3*	Pippa	38.5 × 35.5
4*	A Landscape wc	35.5 × 25.5
5	Landscape with river	17.5 × 12.0
6	The Invincibles (from sketches made in the Four Courts, Dublin) sd 1866	21.5 × 19.5
7*	Judge Whiteside d 1866	19.5 × 19.0
8	Enniscrone, Co. Sligo d 1866	16.0 × 27.0
9	Enniscrone, Co. Sligo d 1866	27.0 × 17.5
10	W. B. as a baby with cat	21.0 × 19.0
11	Mrs. John Butler Yeats d 1867	27.0 × 18.0
12	Young girl	20.5 × 14.0
13	W. B. Yeats as a boy (insc in Lily's handwriting W. B. Yeats)	24.0 × 17.0
14	Anonymous gentleman wc	16.0 × 11.0
15*	Isaac Butt	76.5 × 61.0
16*	Contemporary Club :	
	1 Portraits of Messrs. Arthur Patten and T. W. Russell, M.P.	16.7 × 21.7
	2 Portrait of Mr. Stead of the Mall	7.8 × 7.8
	3 Portrait of Mr. Olohen	16.6 × 13.0
	4 Mr. Baily	16.5 × 7.9
	5 A. Graves, Poet. Plate 12	7.8 × 7.2
	6 Portraits of Mr. Crooks (?) and Mr. Doherty	16.7 × 18.0
	7 Portraits of Mr. Baily (?), Mr. Walker, unknown man, and Mr. Hogg	16.7 × 23.1
	8 Portraits of Mr. G. Coffey and Mr. McNiffe	7.9 × 10.3
	9 Portrait of a man (name indecipherable)	16.7 × 13.4

17	Three girls listening to music (insc J. B. Yeats) wc sd 1883	73.5 × 51.5
18	Three girls listening to music wc	73.5 × 51.5
19	Probably Lily (Susan Mary Yeats) insc J. B. Yeats sd 1884	34.5 × 24.5
20	W. B. Yeats sd 1886	25.0 × 23.0
21*	Contemporary Club :	
	1 W. Morris *Plate 11*	16.8 × 19.0
	2 Prof. Sullivan	16.9 × 11.5
	3 Arnold White	16.8 × 14.6
	4 John O'Leary	16.8 × 22.0
	5 Dr. MacDonnell	16.8 × 11.1
	6 Mr. Taylor	16.8 × 20.3
22	W. B. Yeats with beard (insc W. B. Yeats, Lily's writing) sd	23.0 × 13.5
23	Mrs. Paget insc	15.0 × 23.5
24	Mrs. Paget insc	17.0 × 12.5
25	Mrs. Paget	37.0 × 26.0
26	Mrs. John Butler Yeats	24.0 × 16.5
27	Isaac B. Yeats (brother of artist)	16.5 × 11.5
28	Young girl playing melodeon (crayon)	54.5 × 37.0
29	Two young girls (crayon)	54.5 × 37.0
30	Old man seated	17.0 × 12.0
31	Flying Dutchman (family description)	17.5 × 9.5
32	Lily Yeats (Susan Mary) insc	23.5 × 19.5
33	Lily Yeats (Susan Mary) (insc J. B. Yeats A.R.H.A.)	21.0 × 22.0
34	Elkin Matthews (insc J. B. Yeats) sd 1893	34.5 × 24.5
35*	Douglas Hyde sd 1895	30.0 × 22.5
36*	W. B. Yeats sd 1898	30.5 × 22.5
37	Elizabeth Corbet Yeats (Lolly) insc sd 1898	26.0 × 21.0
38	Cousin Laura Yeats sd 1898	29.0 × 23.0
39	G. W. Russell (AE) sd 1898	30.0 × 23.5
40	Susan Mitchell	28.0 × 22.0
41	Jenny Mitchell	24.5 × 17.0
42	Susan Mitchell insc	27.5 × 21.5
43	W. B. Yeats insc sd 1899	23.5 × 19.5
44	W. B. Yeats insc sd 1899	17.0 × 12.0
45*	Jack B. Yeats sd 1899	26.0 × 21.0
46	Jack B. Yeats insc sd 1899	26.0 × 20.0
47*	Edward Martyn sd 1899 *Plate 15*	28.0 × 22.0
48	Cottie Yeats (Mrs. Jack B. Yeats)	22.0 × 15.5
49*	Kuno Meyer (dated reverse 1900) *Plate 25*	19.0 × 11.0
50	Lady with mandolin d 1900	37.0 × 26.0
51	Lady with mandolin d 1900	25.5 × 36.5
52*	John Eglinton sd 1901 *Plate 23*	29.0 × 21.0
53*	John Eglinton sd 1901	32.0 × 22.0
54	Marian Orr d 1901	26.0 × 19.5

68

55*	Standish O'Grady sd 1902	31.0 × 20.0
56	Norma Borthwick sd 1902	34.5 × 24.5
57	Lily Yeats (Susan Mary) s	23.5 × 18.5
58	Máire Nic Shiubhlaigh s *Plate 30*	24.0 × 23.5
59	Lily (Susan Mary Yeats) wc	21.0 × 22.5
60	John O'Leary	23.5 × 16.5
61	Miss Horniman with a bad cold, alas insc	17.5 × 12.0
62	W. B. Yeats sd 1904	18.5 × 13.0
63	Miss Horniman *Plate 27*	25.0 × 17.0
64	Man and Woman in 'Well of the Saints'	16.5 × 12.5
65	Madame Marcievicz *Plate 20*	24.0 × 17.0
66	Frank Fay *Plate 28*	25.0 × 17.0
67	Keith Strong	23.5 × 15.0
68	Susan Mitchell sd 1905	37.0 × 25.5
69	Anonymous bearded man	30.5 × 23.5
70	Young lady	37.0 × 26.0
71	Patrick Vincent Duffy (1832–1909) sd 1905	25.0 × 18.0
72*	J. M. Synge sd 1905	32.0 × 25.0
73*	Sir Hugh Lane sd 1906 *Plate 14*	19.0 × 15.0
74*	R. I. Best sd 1906	31.0 × 24.0
75	Agnes Tobin insc sd 1906	38.0 × 28.0
76*	Mrs. Best at the piano d 1907	22.0 × 14.0
77*	W. G. Fay sd 1907	17.0 × 13.0
78	Padraic Colum *Plate 21*	35.0 × 26.0
79	Young lady	26.0 × 37.0
80	John Butler Yeats insc wc sd 1907	37.5 × 28.0
81	Portrait of a lady (crayon) sd 1909	56.0 × 46.0
82	Freddy (crayon) insc sd 1909	52.0 × 35.0
83*	J. M. Kerrigan insc sd 1911 *Plate 31*	10.5 × 10.8
84	Mrs. W. B. Yeats insc sd 1920 *Plate 4*	49.5 × 36.0
85*	Ernest Boyd sd 1920 *Plate 26*	50.0 × 36.0
86	Lady insc sd 1921	51.0 × 38.0
87	Lady	51.0 × 38.0
88	Young man seated	51.0 × 37.0
89	Self-Portrait in New York	54.0 × 41.5

PAINTINGS

90	Mrs. Herbert of Muckross Hall	91.0 × 71.0
91*	Portrait of Miss Dowden at the age of 11	76.0 × 63.0
92	Jack in straw hat	31.5 × 25.0
93	Jack in a costume	61.0 × 46.0
94*	Jack B. Yeats as a boy	61.0 × 51.0
95*	Portrait of Mrs. J. B. Yeats *Plate 2*	61.0 × 51.0
96	Lady in red dress (painted in York St. Studio) insc on rere	32.0 × 25.5
97*	The Bird Market s	63.5 × 48.0

98	W. B. Yeats in garden at Bedford Park insc Portrait sketch W. B. Yeats by his father J. B. Yeats, painted in or about 1888–89 in the gardens at 3 Blenheim Rd., Bedford Park, Chiswick, London. In those days W. B. Yeats had a beard. Signed Lily Yeats	61.0 × 46.5
99	Lollie (Elizabeth Corbet Yeats) *Plate 6*	52.0 × 43.5
100	Portrait of a woman	61.0 × 51.0
101	Portrait of a woman	61.0 × 51.0
102	Portrait of a woman	61.0 × 51.0
103	Portrait of a man	61.0 × 51.0
104*	My Daughter s	85.0 × 49.5
105*	Mrs. Heaven (sister of Sir Hugh Lane)	60.0 × 51.5
106*	W. B. Yeats	76.5 × 64.0
107*	Portrait of Frances Elizabeth Geoghegan as a child	46.0 × 36.0
108	Portrait of a man	46.0 × 36.0
109*	Katharine Tynan Hinkson sd 1887 *Plate 16*	
110*	Portrait of Andrew Cullen Tynan	49.0 × 39.0
111*	Violet Osborne Stockley sd 1891	61.0 × 51.0
112*	Portrait of Susan Mitchell sd 1891 *Plate 24*	79.0 × 56.0
113*	Jack B. Yeats sd 1894 *Plate 7*	61.0 × 51.0
114	Lily in white dress sd 1899	76.0 × 63.5
115*	Portrait of W. B. Yeats sd 1900 *Plate 3*	77.0 × 64.0
116*	Portrait of Rosa Butt sd 1900	92.0 × 71.0
117*	Portrait of Miss Lily Yeats sd 1901 *Plate 5*	91.0 × 71.0
118*	Portrait of an old lady sd 1902	66.0 × 51.0
119*	Portrait of Lady Gregory sd 1903 *Plate 13*	62.0 × 52.0
120*	Portrait of George W. Russell (AE) sd 1903 *Plate 19*	112.0 × 87.0
121*	W. G. Fay sd 1904 *Plate 29*	74.0 × 61.5
122*	Lord McDonnell sd 1904	75.0 × 62.0
123*	Portrait of John O'Leary sd 1904 *Plate 9*	112.0 × 87.0
124*	Portrait of Sir Horace Plunkett sd 1904	75.0 × 62.0
125*	Portrait of Standish O'Grady sd 1904 *Plate 10*	112.0 × 87.0
126*	Portrait of George Moore sd 1905 *Plate 17*	77.0 × 64.0
127*	Portrait of Rev. P. S. Dineen sd 1905	77.0 × 64.0
128*	Portrait of Douglas Hyde sd 1906 *Plate 18*	107.0 × 86.0
129*	Dr. Douglas Hyde s	110.0 × 85.0
130*	Mary Lapsley Guest sd 1916	105.0 × 84.0
131*	Portrait of Mary T. L. Caughey sd 1916	102.0 × 71.0
132*	Portrait of Mary T. L. Caughey sd 1916	102.0 × 71.0
133	Mahaffy	76.5 × 63.5
134	George Pollexfen *Plate 8*	91.0 × 71.0
135	Lollie (Elizabeth Corbet Yeats)	91.5 × 71.0
136*	J. M. Synge *Plate 22*	75.0 × 62.5
137	Self-Portrait	76.0 × 63.5
138	Full length self-portrait, commissioned by John Quinn and completed shortly before the artist's death *Plate 1*	152.5 × 102.0

APPENDIX: PICTURES BY JOHN BUTLER YEATS IN OTHER PUBLIC COLLECTIONS IN IRELAND

Size

NATIONAL LIBRARY, Kildare Street, Dublin:

Isaac Butt (pen and ink) d. 1866	10.0 × 11.2
Padraic Colum (pencil)	31.8 × 23.2
Edward Martyn (pencil)	17.0 × 24.2
Susan Mitchell (pencil)	27.2 × 20.8
John O'Leary, George Sigerson (pencil)	16.0 × 25.5
William Pollexfen (pencil) d. 'about 1885'	15.7 × 12.1
Thomas William Rolleston (pencil) d. 1886	16.0 × 22.6
George William Russell (AE) (pencil)	16.5 × 12.0
George William Russell (AE) (pencil)	16.5 × 12.0
John Francis Taylor (pencil)	18.0 × 22.6
John Todhunter (pencil)	21.8 × 13.8
Jack Butler Yeats (pencil)	16.8 × 11.2
Lily Yeats (pencil)	20.5 × 12.2
Lily Yeats (pencil)	23.4 × 18.2
Susan Mary Yeats (Mrs. Yeats in her 24th year) (pencil)	12.0 × 17.4
Susan Mary Yeats (Mrs. Yeats, 1 June 1895) (pencil)	18.8 × 11.0
Susan Mary Yeats (pencil)	22.2 × 14.2
Susan Mary Yeats (pencil)	16.6 × 23.0
William Butler Yeats (pencil)	20.9 × 12.2
William Butler Yeats (pencil)	10.7 × 13.5
William Butler Yeats (pencil)	18.8 × 11.0

ULSTER MUSEUM, Belfast:

Acheson T. Henderson Q. C. (1812-1908) (oil) s.d. 1891	91.5 × 71.5

CRAWFORD ART GALLERY, Cork:

John Redmond (unfinished) (oil)	92.0 × 71.0
Self-Portrait (insc. to John James 1914) (pencil)	18.5 × 33.0

THE ABBEY THEATRE, Dublin:

Máire Nic Shiubhlaigh (oil) s. d. 1904	110.0 × 85.0
Frank Fay (oil) s.d. 1904	110.0 × 85.0
Maire O'Neill (oil) s.d. 1913 NY	109.0 × 86.0
Miss A. Horniman (oil) s.d. 1904	112.0 × 80.0
George William Russell (Æ) (oil)	90.0 × 70.0

DRAWINGS:

Lady Gregory	30.0 × 20.0
A. E. F. Horniman	25.0 × 16.0
Padraic Colum (pencil) s.d. 1905	33.0 × 24.0
J. M. Synge	30.0 × 20.0

SLIGO COUNTY LIBRARY & MUSEUM, Sligo :

DRAWINGS :

	Size
Lily (Susan Mary Yeats), c. 1876–7 (pencil)	13.0 × 19.0
Susan Mitchell (insc) (pencil)	18.0 × 13.0
Susan Mitchell (pencil)	23.0 × 17.0
Jennie Mitchell (pencil) s.d. 1892	22.0 × 15.0
John O'Leary (insc) (pencil)	18.0 × 13.0
Douglas Hyde (insc) (pencil)	17.0 × 12.0
Augusta Gregory (insc) d. 1903	25.0 × 18.0
Padraic Colum (insc) (pencil) d. 1903	25.0 × 18.0
Kuno Meyer (pencil) s.d. 1903	19.0 × 11.0
James Starkey (Seumas O' Sullivan) insc 1903	25.0 × 18.0
Violet Jameson (pencil) s.d. 1906	19.0 × 11.0
Antonio Mancini (insc) (pencil) s	16.0 × 10.0
George Pollexfen	
Lily (Susan Mary Yeats (insc) (pencil) s.d. 1908	34.0 × 23.0
Recollection of No. 23 T.C.D. 1902 (pencil) (insc)	7.0 × 12.0
Self-Portrait (insc) (pencil) s.d. 1921	21.0 × 15.0
Lily (Susan Mary Yeats (pencil)	17.0 × 12.0

OIL :

	Size
Self-Portrait (oil on board), c. 1916	35.0 × 47.0

(For works in The National Gallery of Ireland or The Municipal Gallery of Modern Art Dublin see pp. 67-70.)

ACKNOWLEDGEMENTS

Acknowledgement is given

to Senator Michael Yeats and Anne Yeats for permission to quote from the works of W. B. Yeats and John Butler Yeats and to reproduce drawings and paintings by John Butler Yeats;

to Mr. Emmet Green for quotations from the works of Padraic Colum;

to Professor William M. Murphy for quotations from The Yeats Family and the Pollexfens of Sligo;

to Professor William M. Murphy, Executor of the Estate of Jeanne Robert Foster for permission to quote 'Alas for the Wonderful Yew Forest'.